MACHINES AT WORK

Motorbikes

Clive Gifford

 Crabtree Publishing Company
www.crabtreebooks.com

Crabtree Publishing Company
www.crabtreebooks.com
1-800-387-7650

PMB 59051, 350 Fifth Ave.   616 Welland Ave.
59th Floor,   St. Catharines, ON
New York, NY 10118   L2M 5V6

Published by Crabtree Publishing in 2013

Author: Clive Gifford
Editors: Nicola Edwards, Adrianna Morganelli
Proofreaders: Wendy Scavuzzo, Crystal Sikkens
Designer: Elaine Wilkinson
Picture Researcher: Clive Gifford
**Production coordinator and
    Prepress technician**: Ken Wright
Print coordinator: Katherine Berti

To find out about the author, visit his website:
www.clivegifford.co.uk

First published in 2012 by Wayland
(A division of Hachette Children's Books)
Copyright © Wayland 2012

Printed in Hong Kong/ 092012/BK20120629

Picture acknowledgements:
The author and publisher would like to thank
the following for allowing their pictures to
be reproduced in this publication: Cover
(main) Julie Lucht / Shutterstock.com, (inset)
asiana / Shutterstock.com; title page Stephen
Mcsweeny / Shutterstock.com; pp2-3 taelove7
/ Shutterstock.com; p4 Getty Images; p5
(t) Shutterstock © Lola, (b) 7382489561 /
Shutterstock.com; p6 Mark Yuill / Shutterstock.
com; p7 (t) Shutterstock © Katrina Brown,
(b) Shutterstock © Jordache; p8 taelove7 /
Shutterstock.com; p9 (t) iStock © Damir
Spanic, (b) Tupungato / Shutterstock.com;
p10 (t) Stephen Mcsweeny / Shutterstock.
com, (b) Red_hayabusa / Shutterstock.com;
p11 Giovanna Tondelli / Shutterstock.com; p12
Getty Images; p13 (t) Shutterstock © azaphoto,
(b) Alvin Ganesh / Shutterstock.com; p14
mobil11 / Shutterstock.com; p15 (t) iStock
© graham heywood, (b) iStock © 4X-image;
p16 Pospisil MRL / Shutterstock.com; p17
(t) DSPA / Shutterstock.com, (b) KuuLeeR
/ Shutterstock.com; p18 Graham Prentice /
Shutterstock.com; p19 Shutterstock © risteski
goce; p20 Jordan Tan / Shutterstock.com; p21
(t) Thomas Bedenk / Shutterstock.com, (b) jan
kranendonk / Shutterstock.com; p22 (t) Pospisil
MRL / Shutterstock.com, (b) Mark Yuill /
Shutterstock.com; p23 mobil11 / Shutterstock.
com; p24 Pospisil MRL / Shutterstock.com

**Library and Archives Canada
Cataloguing in Publication**

CIP available at Library and Archives Canada

**Library of Congress
Cataloging-in-Publication Data**

CIP available at Library of Congress

Contents

Motorbikes on the move

Motorbikes and motorcycles are vehicles that run on two wheels. Most motorcycles are larger and heavier than motorbikes. Both have an engine that burns **fuel** to provide the power that turns the wheels. As the wheels turn, the vehicle travels forward. Many motorbikes and motorcycles are used for work, but some are ridden for fun or to compete in races.

Rider grips handlebars

FAST FACT

There are over 200 million motorbikes in use. Over half of these are in Asia.

Front wheel covered in a rubber tire

ZOOM IN

Most motorbikes use a chain to move, a lot like the one on your bicycle. The engine pulls on the chain, which then turns the motorbike's back wheel.

Motorbikes are used all over the world as a cheap form of transportation. Most cost much less to build and run than cars. They can be used to deliver items quickly to customers. Motorbikes can be fitted with different racks and attachments to carry things.

Rider sits on seat

This powerful machine races on tracks at speeds of over 186 miles per hour (299 kilometers per hour)

Engine underneath this covering is called a fairing

A motorbike rider delivers farm produce in India.

Engine power

A motorbike's engine burns fuel. The burning fuel creates gases that move parts inside the engine. Most motorbikes have smaller engines than cars. Motorbikes are smaller and lighter in weight, so they do not need as much engine power to move.

The engine is cooled by air traveling past it.

Exhaust pipe

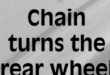

FAST FACT

The Triumph Rocket III's motorcycle engine is huge! It is almost twice the size of the engines used in many small cars.

Chain turns the rear wheel

Fuel tank stores liquid fuel

ZOOM IN

Burning fuel creates waste gases. Metal tubes called **exhaust pipes** carry these gases away from the engine and out behind the motorbike.

Most motorbikes are started by the rider turning a key to fire up the engine. To start some older model motorbikes, riders have to press a foot pedal down sharply. This is called a kick start.

Rubber tires grip the road

To start this motorbike, the rider turns an ignition key.

Steering

A rider steers a motorbike using handlebars in a similar way to riding a bicycle. When riders want to steer around a bend or corner, they turn the handlebars. The front wheel turns, and the rest of the bike follows in the same direction.

Turning a sharp corner, these racers lean their bikes into the bend. They will move back into an upright position as they complete their turn.

ZOOM IN

These orange lights are called turn signals. When a rider wants to turn, the left or right light flashes to let other vehicles know the direction the motorbike is going to turn.

Whether riders are on busy roads or on racing tracks, they must check that there are no obstacles or other vehicles in their way before they make a turn.

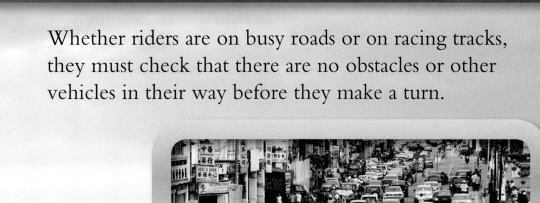

Motorbikes are small and can turn easily to weave in and out of busy city traffic. This allows couriers to deliver packages fast and other motorcyclists to get to work quickly.

Speeding up

The right-hand grip on a motorbike's handlebars is called the **throttle**. When a rider twists the throttle, the engine works harder and sends more power to the rear wheel. This makes the motorbike go faster.

This is called a wheelie. The rider increases the engine power sharply. The rear wheel thrusts forward and the front wheel lifts off the ground.

ZOOM IN

This dial is called a **speedometer**. It tells a rider how fast the motorbike is going. Riders have to make sure they do not break the speed limit on a road.

Motorbikes at work often have to travel fast. Couriers sometimes have to speed up and change lanes to pass slower vehicles. Police motorcyclists may have to go even faster to catch speeding cars or to race to the scene of a crime.

FAST FACT

The Suzuki Hayabusa motorcycle can speed up faster than most other motorcycles. It can move from a standstill to 62 mph (100 km/h) in under three seconds.

This police motorcyclist speeds through town to answer an emergency call.

Riding safely

Unlike car drivers, motorbike riders do not have a frame around them to protect them if they crash. They have to wear protective clothing in case they fall off their motorbike.

Crash helmet—cushions and protects head

Padded leather gloves—protects hands

This rider crashed and was thrown from his motorbike. He was protected by his safety clothing and walked away unharmed.

Motorcycle boots have steel toecaps

Pads on knees are called knee sliders

Motorbike riders use their brakes to slow down or stop when trying to avoid a bump or crash. To make the brakes work, riders squeeze levers that are attached to the handlebars.

FAST FACT

The Honda Gold Wing motorcycle was the first to be fitted with an airbag. (The airbag is located in front of the rider and blows up like a balloon if the motorcycle crashes).

ZOOM IN

The brake disk is attached to the motorbike's wheel. When the brakes are used, pads press against the disk. This creates a force called **friction**, which slows the motorbike's wheel down.

Riders have used their brakes to stop on this busy road in Vietnam.

Off-road riding

Many motorbikes are used to travel off-road, or over rough, bumpy, sandy, or muddy ground. They are useful because they are able to go places other vehicles cannot. Some, for example, are used to rescue injured walkers or climbers on hills.

Rider wears a full-face crash helmet

Mudguard stops dirt off the front tire from hitting the rider

This off-road racing motorbike has a strong frame that can take a heavy landing after a jump.

Long seat where the rider sits

Race number

Many off-road motorbikes are raced in **motocross** competitions. These are exciting races for as many as 40 bikes. Competitors ride laps around a short dirt and mud course that has many bumps and jumps.

Two motocross riders race side by side over a dirt course.

ZOOM IN

This spring and tube device is called a shock absorber. It helps to absorb some of the bumps felt by a rider when they travel over rough ground or land after a jump.

Motorbike racing

Some motorbikes are raced on twisting and turning tracks that are covered with a smooth surface like a road. MotoGP bikes are the fastest track motorbikes. These machines are built just for racing.

Top racer Valentino Rossi rides his MotoGP motorbike. Rossi hunches low, creating a **streamlined** shape. This allows the bike to go faster.

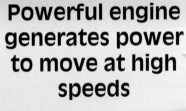

Powerful engine generates power to move at high speeds

Large, smooth rubber tires grip the track

ZOOM IN

MotoGP bikes are fitted with a covering at the front called a fairing. The fairing helps to smooth the flow of air around the bike, increasing its speed.

Speedway races take place on short, oval-shaped dirt tracks. Four riders take part in each race. Riders slide their motorbikes sideways into corners. They speed up to 68 mph (109 km/h) on the straight parts of the track.

Two speedway riders race around a dirt track. They control their speed using the throttle only. These motorbikes do not have brakes!

Carrying loads

As well as carrying their riders and sometimes passengers, motorbikes and motorcycles can be used to carry other objects. Racks bolted onto the frame allow boxes and bags to be attached. This means riders can carry and deliver a variety of loads from pizzas to medical supplies.

Windshield

This motorcycle is designed for traveling long distances. It is large, has a comfortable seat and riding position, and plenty of places to store things.

ZOOM IN

A **pannier** is a bag or solid box that sits over the rear wheel and can be filled with tools and other things a rider needs to carry with them.

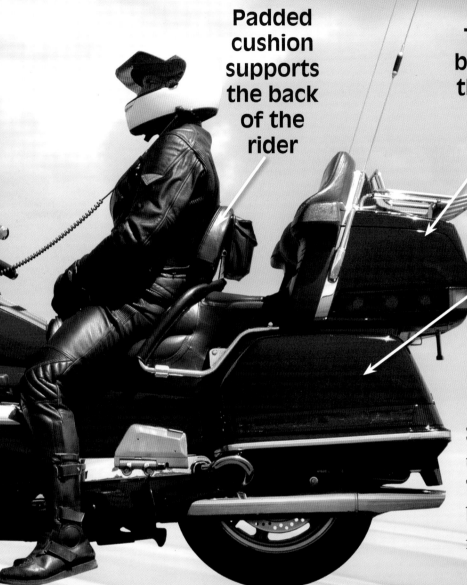

Padded cushion supports the back of the rider

Top box is bolted onto the back of bike

Pannier stores spare clothing and supplies

Some motorcycles are three-wheeled vehicles. The extra wheel at the back gives a stable base for carrying bigger loads.

A motorcycle sidecar is a pod containing a seat for an extra passenger. The sidecar is supported by its own wheel. This helps to keep the motorcycle balanced.

Emergency bikes

Motorcycles are used by emergency services to reach fires, accidents, and crime scenes more quickly than cars and trucks. They can travel fast down narrow streets and are easy to stop and park. The rider can get off the motorcycle quickly to help an injured person or chase a suspect on foot.

Police motorcycles can cruise at slow speeds when they are on patrol. Here, a group of police officers on motorcycles set off on traffic patrol in Singapore.

Bright headlight for riding at night

Storage boxes hold tools and first-aid kit

ZOOM IN

Some police motorcycles have a large flashing light at the back to warn other motorists they are approaching. The light is switched on and off by a button on the handlebars.

A motorcycle carries a **battery** that powers its lights and other electrical devices. Emergency motorcycles may have a second battery to power extra lights, sound speakers, and other equipment.

Motorcycle ambulances race paramedics with emergency medical supplies to the scene of an accident.

FAST FACT

Firefighters are testing out special fire bikes. The motorcycles are fitted with their own tanks of water and a hose 98 feet (30 meters) long.

Quiz

How much have you found out about motorbikes at work? Try this short quiz!

1. Which continent is home to over half of all the world's motorbikes?
a) Europe
b) Asia
c) North America

2. Which control does the rider use to speed up the motorbike?
a) throttle
b) ignition
c) brakes

3. MotoGP bikes are raced on what sort of course?
a) a dirt oval
b) over cross country
c) on smooth tracks

4. What part of a motorbike uses friction between two parts to slow a motorbike down?
a) brakes
b) steering
c) throttle

5. Which type of motorbike has no brakes and is raced on dirt tracks?
a) MotoGP
b) speedway
c) motocross

6. Where would you find knee sliders?
a) in the motorbike's engine
b) on the motorbike's handlebars
c) as part of a rider's racing clothing

7. Which motorbike was the first to have an airbag installed?
a) Honda Gold Wing
b) Suzuki Hayabusa
c) Honda Super Cub

8. How much time does it take a Suzuki Hayabusa to move from a standstill to 62 mph (100 km/h)?
a) under one second
b) under two seconds
c) under three seconds

Answers: 1.b, 2.a, 3.c, 4.a, 5.b, 6.c, 7.a, 8.c

Glossary

battery A device that supplies power to the electrical parts of a motorbike

crash helmet A protective head covering worn by motorbike riders to stop head injuries if they crash

exhaust pipes Metal tubes that move waste gases away from a motorbike's engine

fairing A covering at the front of a motorbike that protects the rider from wind and helps make the motorbike more streamlined

friction The force that slows movement between two objects that rub together

fuel Gasoline, diesel, or another substance burned in an engine to create power to make a motorbike move

fuel tank A container, usually made of metal, that holds the motorbike's fuel

motocross Motorcycle races around laps of a bumpy dirt course

pannier A storage container that rests on either side of the rear wheel

speedometer A dial or electronic screen that displays a motorbike's speed

streamlined Describes something that is shaped so that air travels easily and smoothly over or around it

throttle The control on the right-hand grip of a motorbike's handlebars that changes the speed of the engine

Further information

Books

Sport Bikes, Katharine Bailey, Crabtree Publishing, 2007
Street Bikes, Rachel Eagen, Crabtree Publishing, 2007
Motocross History, Bob Woods, Crabtree Publishing, 2008
Extreme Motocross, Bobbie Kalman and John Crossingham,
Crabtree Publishing, 2004

Websites

Bill's Old Bike Barn: www.billsbikebarn.com/index.php?pageid=3&gallery=VintageBikes&wd=750px&show=5
This site has nearly 40 photographs of vintage motorcycles.

Honda Powersports: http://powersports.honda.com/
This site features dozens of photographs of Honda street bikes, including touring, cruisers, choppers, and off-road bikes.

Supercross: www.supercross.com/
This site has race results, details about top riders, dozens of photographs of races, and a few videos.

Speedway Bikes: www.speedwaybikes.com/rw/index.htm
This part of the site features dozens of riders. It gives details about each rider and has photographs of the person in action.

The LeMay – America's Car Museum, Tacoma, Washington, U.S.A. www.lemaymuseum.org
Featuring more than 500 cars, this museum showcases cars for their speed, design, and technology, as well their importance to car culture.

Gilmore Car Museum, Michigan, U.S.A. www.gilmorecarmuseum.org
This museum houses a collection of classic cars, including muscle cars and alternative fuel cars.

Index